MANNERS THAT MATTER MOST

THE EASY GUIDE TO ETIQUETTE
AT HOME AND IN THE WORLD

MANNERS THAT MATTER MOST

THE EASY GUIDE TO ETIQUETTE AT HOME AND IN THE WORLD

RESEARCHED AND WRITTEN BY
JUNE EDING

WITH A SPECIAL FOREWORD BY
NORAH LAWLOR

hatherleigh

Manners That Matter Most
Text copyright © 2014 Hatherleigh Press

Library of Congress Cataloging-in-Publication Data is available
upon request.
ISBN: 978-1-57826-518-3

Cover and Interior Design by Carolyn Kasper

Printed in the United States
10 9 8 7 6 5 4 3 2

CONTENTS

FOREWORD

W HY DO MANNERS matter?
Some would say that books offering
guidance in matters of etiquette such as
Emily Post and Debrett's are outdated for
the modern world. However, I would sug-
gest that the modern world is precisely why
good manners and the practice of etiquette
matters even more today. In an era where
a message placed online can be transmitted
world-wide and where modern cities are cul-
tural melting pots comprised of people from
many different nationalities, all with their
own customs, the opportunity for making
social errors is multiplied many fold.

Good manners are in short supply today,
not necessarily because people are less cour-
teous, but because sources of guidance that
are relevant to modern lifestyles and language are harder to come by. *Manners That
Matter Most* is an important contribution as
it takes an old subject and presents it in a

fresh and accessible way. This book reminds us why good practice in etiquette not only makes the practitioner look good, but also helps reinforce a sense of social structure which in the end makes life simpler, better communicated, and less stressful.

Good individual etiquette has a role at the larger level of society—if we were to all practice good manners, would not the world simply be a nicer place?

—NORAH LAWLOR

INTRODUCTION

*Friends and good manners will
carry you where money won't go.*
—Margaret Walker

F OR PEOPLE WITH good manners, doors
are constantly opening.

Well-mannered people turn chance meetings into rewarding relationships. They ap-
proach formal events or stressful meetings
with less anxiety and more confidence. They
navigate life's twists and turns successfully,
maintaining control and keeping perspective
on what matters.

This is because behaving with consideration toward others—the guiding tenet of
good manners—has multiple benefits. As we
go through our days, the simple practice of
showing kindness to each other, like saying
"please" and "thank you," showing up on

time, and getting back to someone promptly, goes a long way. Good manners help us make a good impression, provide us with structure and reassurance, and help us get through life's rough spots with aplomb.

The goal of good manners is not perfection. In fact, good manners guide us when we do something wrong or when things don't turn out as planned. When it's time to make an apology, good manners help us communicate sincerely. When someone else is rude to us, being polite helps us handle the situation so it doesn't get worse.

We all make mistakes, and life is unpredictable. When life throws us a curveball, good manners make the ups and downs easier to handle.

PART I

WHY DO GOOD MANNERS MATTER?

Manners are a sensitive awareness of the feelings of others. If you have that awareness, you have good manners, no matter what fork you use.

—Emily Post

THE WORD "MANNERS" may cause some of us to think back to childhood, when boring lessons were enforced by a strict older relative or we were scolded at the dinner table.

In fact, manners aren't about being told how to dress, speak, or act. Being well mannered doesn't require knowledge of a hundred different rules. We shouldn't worry that having good manners means "going back" to a bygone era when people were uptight, judgmental, and used decorum as a means to judge and ostracize others.

Having good manners means being kind. It means considering someone else's viewpoint alongside your own.

The core of good manners is the golden rule: "Treat others as you yourself would want to be treated."

MANNERS MAKE LIFE EASIER

*Civility costs nothing and
buys everything.*

—Mary Wortley Montagu

———•◦•———

Having good manners means treating other people with kindness and respect. It doesn't take much, but small actions make a big difference. In the course of a busy day, simple gestures reassure the people we interact with that we are taking them into consideration and doing what we can to make things more pleasant. For those we know and love, employing good manners solidifies our relationship and shows others how much we appreciate them.

These small kindnesses make our lives easier. They take the anxiety out of living in a world where we are constantly meeting new people and encountering new faces. They help make our relationships at home, at work, and among friends more rewarding.

Manners are also reassuring. We can rely on the common language of manners in any situation. When we walk into a party where we don't know anyone, manners make us confident that we will make a good impression. Manners also help us overcome potential awkwardness when we bump into a stranger, and alleviate anxiety at meeting a friend's family for the first time.

Manners are guideposts for behavior that serve as helpful road signs on the path of human interaction.

We can't anticipate other people's needs *all* the time, or know with absolute certainty what someone else wants. But when it comes to social situations and spending time with each other, we share the same basic desires:

we all want to feel accepted, respected, and put at ease so we can have a good time in a new situation or meet our objective quickly and efficiently. We don't want to feel rushed or bossed, put on the spot, or unappreciated or ignored.

Practicing good manners doesn't have to be complicated.

Simple actions make a big impact. Show up on time (or apologize sincerely if we're late), serve someone else before we serve ourselves at a table, or hold the door open for someone if their hands are full. These actions form a portrait in someone else's mind of who we really are: a considerate, thoughtful person.

Having good manners means understanding that we all want respect and kindness, and striving to do what we can to ensure other people are treated well. Being a well-mannered person means you have a wealth of tools available to make any situation easier.

THE POWER OF A FIRST IMPRESSION

*A man's manners are a mirror in
which he shows his portrait.*

—Johann Wolfgang von Goethe

————•◦•————

When it comes to making a good impression, our most powerful tool isn't a power suit, expensive watch, or statement jewelry. Good manners cost us nothing, are readily accessible at any time, and no matter what we're wearing, guarantee we will stand out in a crowd.

People with good manners set themselves apart in person, on the phone, and online. A well-mannered adult stands out as a person with "something special" whom other people want to be around. In matters professional and personal, people with good manners are welcomed into other people's lives as friends, coworkers, trusted allies, and long-term partners.

Whether it's a job interview, first date, or meeting important family members for the first time, good manners put us on the fast-track to being appreciated and respected by someone whom we've only just met.

Being kind and considerate to one another, in a variety of ways for a variety of circumstances, plants the seeds of a relationship. With good manners on display, we can turn an initial meeting into a friendship or long-term relationship, and ensure that the best of who we are is visible.

A MORE PROFOUND BENEFIT

Class is considerate of others. It knows that good manners are nothing more than a series of petty sacrifices.

—Ann Landers

At first, learning to pay attention to the needs of someone else may seem like a burden.

In fact, considering another person's viewpoint and striving to treat him or her with respect in turn provides an opportunity to forget our own problems and preoccupations.

Manners can liberate us from churning worries and anxious internal chatter. They can even help us to find a way out of a bad mood. They allow us to shift perspective from our own internal struggles and dramas to being in the present moment with another person. In the process, we can learn something new about someone we hadn't met before and take a break from our own inner dilemmas. Often, we emerge from our interaction to discover that whatever issue or problem we were so caught up with in the first place doesn't really matter in the grand scheme of things.

HOW TO USE THIS BOOK

This book won't tell you how to use a fish fork, or what wording to use on a wedding invitation, or how to choose between sending flowers or a card, and so on. Although these pages offer specific tips and suggestions, *Manners That Matter Most* is not about providing you with strict rules for how to behave.

Rather, it is intended as a reminder of the benefits of practicing good manners. Far from a strict "do's and don'ts" list of behavior and decorum, good manners open opportunities to us, turn good first impressions into friendships, and help us experience the world as an enjoyable place on a daily basis. They provide a reassuring structure we can return to when things are hectic at home or at work. They allow us to offer the best of ourselves. This process can be incredibly rewarding. Often, making someone else's day makes our day, too.

We have many demands on our time. But cultivating good manners doesn't have to be hard work. This book covers 25 essentials applicable to any situation—at work, at home, and among friends and acquaintances—that are easy to incorporate into your daily life. With a little bit of effort and consistent practice, they will help you turn good manners into a habit you will maintain over a lifetime.

PART II

INCORPORATING GOOD MANNERS INTO MODERN LIFE

In matters of style, swim with the current; in matters of principle, stand like a rock.

—Thomas Jefferson

WE LEAD TREMENDOUSLY busy lives. Technology has made our lives easier, but it has also complicated them. Every day, cell phones, email, and a buzzing online world compete for our attention. Meanwhile, the demands of work, friends and family pull at our priorities.

Under these circumstances, the act of incorporating good manners into our lives may seem more challenging than ever. In truth, good manners are simple: They center on respecting those around us, as well as ourselves.

The golden rule hasn't changed in thousands of years, and it is with good reason that we are called to act kindly toward one another.

A BRIEF HISTORY OF ETIQUETTE

Providing people with guidance on how to benefit the most from society and their relationships is an ancient practice. Good manners, ethics, and practicing kindness toward each other are deeply rooted in human history, going back through the centuries and encompassing cultures around the world.

As far back as 551–479 BCE, the Chinese philosopher, politician and teacher Confucius developed a philosophy that placed its main emphasis on morality, justice, maintaining correct relationships, sincerity, family loyalty, and respect. He encouraged others to live by a code of moral behavior similar to that of the golden rule, that of *"Do not do to others what you do not want done to yourself."*

By 25–24 BCE, an ancient Egyptian official named Ptahhotep wrote *The Maxims of Ptahhotep* (believed by many scholars to be the first book ever written). The Maxims provided guidelines for behavior and social conduct, covering everything from table manners to tips for maintaining peaceful relationships, and encouraging the development of key virtues, including self-control and kindness toward others.

As the centuries passed and civilization established itself around the world, political dealings, social climbing, and the struggle to find a place of favor at the royal court fostered etiquette, a strict code of behavior that is not synonymous with manners. The word "etiquette" (from the French *etiquette*, meaning "tag" or "label") was picked up by the English language around 1750. Although, for some, practicing good manners means adhering to etiquette, etiquette and good manners are not the same thing. Whereas good manners focuses on considering others and being kind, etiquette turns a sharp critical eye to one's own behavior, enforcing standards for how to dress, speak and act—with strict penalties. During the late 17th century, the period of the Enlightenment in Europe, identifying oneself as a member of the elite required following a code of sophisticated behaviors. Rules of etiquette became precise and unyielding; there were specific times when it was appropriate to show emotion, for example. Although smiling was acceptable, laughing was considered to be "characteristic of folly and ill-manners." "It is the manner in which the mob express their silly joy at silly things," wrote the 4th Earl of Chesterfield, Philip Stanhope, who first used the word "etiquette" as we know it today. By the Victorian era (1837-1901), etiquette had become a complicated web of rules, applicable to every interaction between people, as well as actions such as writing letters and using cutlery.

But as time wore on, these rules gave way. Periods of social upheaval challenged class structure. Individual expression became more important than a code of behavior. Now, we live in a completely new era.

MANNERS AND MODERN LIFE

Today, the convenience of modern technology presents us with a unique challenge.

We live in an era when it is socially acceptable to enter a virtual realm and more or less remove ourselves from the world around us. People can shop while listening to music, chat on their cell phones with someone miles away, and send emails and texts while waiting in line or walking down the street.

Although it may certainly be convenient to have 24-hour access to an online universe, more and more often they are leading us to behave poorly toward one another at home, at work, in social situations, and on the go.

No matter how complicated our lives may be, we can still learn to uphold the basic tenets of good manners. We can weave polite behavior into our days and still accomplish what we need to get done.

It starts with an understanding of what unique challenges we face at home, at work, and in a fast-paced world.

CHALLENGES TO MAINTAINING GOOD MANNERS AT HOME, AT WORK, AND IN A TECHNOLOGICAL WORLD

AT HOME

Maintaining good manners at home can sometimes be more challenging than practicing them in the world at large.

It's all too easy to fall into the trap of assuming that, because a spouse or partner, roommate, or family member likes or loves us, we can skip all formalities and forgo good manners altogether. We may even excuse our own bad behavior and write off our negative habits by calling them "quirks" that those who love us must accept as "part of who I am." Of course, this isn't true. No one is given a blank check to behave however they want in front anyone, family member or not.

Other times, we sacrifice considerate behavior for the sake of personal convenience. This may happen without us even realizing it. For example, we may find ourselves shouting a question at someone from across the house because we're impatient to take care of something. Or, we may skip saying "please" and "thank you," and revert to issuing demands in our efforts to get everyone out the door on time.

These slip-ups are certainly understandable, but they take advantage of our relationships with others. They can also lead to hurt feelings and cause strain and negativity, causing a ripple effect of resentment. In a frantic moment, it may seem okay to boss someone around in the interest of making things happen faster, but injuring someone with a curt word takes longer to fix than being polite in the first place.

Taking the time and making a conscious effort to treat roommates, loved ones, and family members with the same respect we would give to a person we're meeting for the first time ensures that life at home is pleasant for everyone.

Furthermore, the structure provided by codes of behavior is reassuring: Everyone in the household is held accountable to the same standards of behavior, and no one is exempt. When people feel respected and are enjoying a calmer environment, they are more likely to contribute to daily tasks and chores, leading to an efficient household. In a home environment that is prone to becoming hectic, manners keep us grounded in what really matters: being good to each other.

TREATING FAMILY MEMBERS AND ROOMMATES WITH RESPECT

We often forget that the people we live with deserve the same level of respect and consideration as those whom we meet in more formal settings.

Here are some helpful manners to keep in mind at home:

- Don't speak to someone when they are behind closed doors (this includes the bathroom).
- Don't yell across the house.
- Say "please" and "thank you."
- If you'd like them to turn down their music or you need to remind them to complete a shared task, ask politely.
- Take care to acknowledge someone else's efforts. If they took out the garbage or did the dishes, take the time to let them know you noticed what they did and thank them. Maintaining a clean house is constant work and everyone's efforts, whether big or small, should be appreciated.

AT WORK

It is often said that, "It's not personal; it's just business."

The world of business is ever-changing. It is constantly responding to any number of outside forces, from a fluctuating world market and a shifting economy, to the pace of technology and manufacturing, to trends, seasonal demands, and even unpredictable celebrity influence and the tides of social media. Under these circumstances, no organization or company can remain stagnant. The result is change. Clients, deals, plans, proposals, assignments; all are subjected to last-minute readjustments and cancellations. In these cases, it's not personal; it's business.

However, "it's not personal, it's business" should never be used as a blanket justification for mistreating coworkers or employees. While the changing tides of business may not be personal, the workplace is. An office is a place where relationships and respect between coworkers and management make or break a company's long-term success. Maintaining harmony in a department *despite* big changes is vital to a successful workday and a productive workforce. In the close quarters of the office setting, where people can spend more time working with each other than they do with loved ones or family, maintaining a code of manners is essential. Passing stress down the line, so to speak, only contributes to a stymied, inefficient workplace fueled by anxiety, anger, and resentment.

Use manners to keep things in check. The simple use of phrases like "please," "thank you," and/or other acknowledgments like "I appreciate that" helps to foster good will. It also assists employees and coworkers in feeling that their efforts are acknowledged, and creates a working environment where people naturally strive to offer their best and feel inspired to be a part of that environment for years to come.

USING TECHNOLOGY POLITELY

Technology is changing how we interact with each other in leaps and bounds. With smart phones nearly everywhere, anyone can have access to a virtual world, 24/7. We are being forced to answer the question: How do we live in one world together, while simultaneously spending time in a virtual reality?

For many, the answer is: We can't. If we want to enjoy each other's company and fully experience life in the moment, our use of technology has to be structured and compartmentalized.

Of course, many would argue that "when in Rome, do as the Romans do"; in other words, if someone is on their phone checking email, you can, too. There is some truth to this perspective. However, we still risk being taken out of our experience of the present moment, and the possible interactions we could enjoy with those around us, when we give in to the distraction of text, email, or the Internet. There are also real, undeniable risks: texting while driving causes car crashes every year, and pedestrians who aren't paying attention to their surroundings because of their phone may injure others or walk right into an accident.

Remember, you're in control of technology, not the other way around. In most cases, you don't have to answer a text message or email immediately. If you are hanging out with friends or loved ones, take a break from your phone. You work hard at your job to have free time, and you have a right to enjoy it. Remind yourself that you set aside the time to be with those close to you; take full advantage of that time before it's over. The time we spend with each other doesn't come back again.

If you find yourself debating whether or not jumping onto your phone is appropriate, keep this rule in mind:

Modern technology does not provide you with the excuse to be late, act rude, ignore others, or distance yourself from the world in a manner that is inconsiderate. If you find yourself doing so, put your phone or head-phones away, and start paying attention to the world around you and your role within it.

PART III

25 ESSENTIALS TO GOOD MANNERS

THIS SECTION OF the book covers 25 essentials of good manners. This isn't a comprehensive list of do's and don'ts. Rather, this section is meant to provide you with helpful guidance and reminders. It's designed to help you think in terms of what it means to act with good manners in mind—with kindness and consideration toward others—every day. These tips cover situations with a variety of people, from strangers to coworkers, family members, and partners. These are principles that you can practice every day so that, over time, good manners will become an ingrained habit that you don't have to think twice about.

1

TAKE THE TIME TO BE POLITE: DON'T RUSH

WHEN OUR LIVES get hectic, busy, and stressful, manners can be the first thing to go. This is a mistake.

We shouldn't assume that being polite takes up too much time to be worth the trouble. Being considerate of others adds mere seconds to a conversation. And, in the long run, taking a bit more time to express ourselves clearly and respectfully, and listen attentively to another person, saves us time and effort.

Behaving politely and striving to listen and work *with* someone else, rather than against them, helps us achieve our desired outcome with ease and efficiency. Good manners facilitate clear communication and save us time overall. In contrast, bossing others and demanding what we want can lead to confusion at best; hurt feelings, resentment, and retaliation at worse. When we injure others, we have to take the time to repair the relationship.

In all that you do, strive to take the time to be polite and kind to another person, whether it's a stranger, coworker, or family member. If you're getting worked up, take a deep breath before you speak to the other person. Sometimes just a second to remember that the person we're speaking with is human, just like us, reminds us to behave with kindness. Approaching our relationships with sensitivity for others benefits us in the long run.

Life is not so short but
that there is always time
enough for courtesy.
—RALPH WALDO EMERSON

2

CONSIDER YOUR APPEARANCE

"CONSIDERING YOUR appearance" doesn't mean dressing or acting a certain way to fit in. It simply means visualizing how you appear to others. If we aren't aware of our mood and how it's being projected to others, it can work against us. This is because our facial expressions and body language speak volumes before we have the chance to utter a single word.

If you show up to an event scowling over a long commute, the people who see you when you walk in the door won't know why you look disgruntled; they'll just see your unpleasant expression. Your explanation about bad traffic or subway delays won't undo their first impression. Your body language will have already done the talking.

Before you walk into the door to meet someone else, take a quick inventory of how you feel and how others might see you. Are you feeling stressed, hurried, or rushed? Do you *look* stressed, hurried, or rushed? What mood do you project?

You may *feel* anxious, tired, or nervous about an encounter; the trick is to avoid communicating that bad mood to others. Stand up straight. Take a few deep breaths. Make the effort to feel relaxed and at ease, if possible. Smile to show that you are welcoming and open to others. The objective is to showcase how happy you are to see the people you're meeting from the very first moment you enter the room.

After all, "You only have one chance to make a first impression." More importantly, you only have one chance to communicate that you are genuinely pleased to see someone.

Clothes and manners do not
make the man; but, when
he is made, they greatly
improve his appearance.

—HENRY WARD BEECHER

3

BE ON TIME

THE WAY YOU show up to an event or
social gathering sends a strong message.
When you're on time, you communicate that
you respect the other person and their time,
and that you're invested in sharing your
time with them, too. This makes punctuality
one of the easiest ways to give someone else
a positive impression of you. It's also a great
way to set the stage for an enjoyable or productive meeting.

When it comes to parties, being on time
shows that you respect the host or hostess
and conveys your enthusiasm for being there
more effectively than any gift.

When meeting a friend, being on time
saves you both the hassle of phone calls,
emails, and text messages with updates on
your impending arrival. It also avoids putting your friend in the awkward position of

having to wait at a bar or restaurant, alone, for you to arrive.

At work, punctuality conveys that you value the time of others, and that you are also someone who takes your own time—and yourself—seriously. Being on time communicates your professionalism and your dedication to your job.

Being on time requires planning, but it isn't difficult. Take advantage of this easy opportunity to make a positive impression and start off your time with someone else on the right foot.

People count up the faults of
those who keep them waiting.

—FRENCH PROVERB

Gratitude is not only the greatest of virtues, but the parent of all the others.

—MARCUS TULLIUS CICERO

4

EXPRESS GRATITUDE
THE RIGHT WAY

THANKING SOMEONE for their thoughtfulness sets you apart as a considerate person and good friend.

In some ways, saying "thank you" is easier than ever. We have a range of communication at our fingertips almost 24 hours a day: We can tap out a text message, type an email, send a handwritten note, or make a phone call. There's no reason to hold back your expression of gratitude. Each means of getting in touch is sized to fit the breadth of your "thank you" and the nature of your relationship with the recipient.

When crafting your thank you, consider who is receiving your message and what means of communication they would most appreciate. For a close friend who's always texting, a text message thanking her for coming to your party, which she can read when she's arrived home or when she's out the next day, will be appreciated. For an older friend of the family, a handwritten note is probably most appropriate. For a long-distance friend, a call or letter may offer a more intimate way to connect across the miles between you.

Whether you send a handwritten note, an e-mail, or brief text message, make sure your "thank you" is just that: an expression of gratitude that acknowledges the other person's gift, kind actions, or words. Keep it simple and focus your message on how much you appreciate what the other person did for you.

A warning: Simplicity can be challenging when thanking someone via email. More casual than letter writing, email skips formality and tempts us to go on at length, lumping separate topics of conversation together. We may start the email with a thank you, only to go on and ask for a favor or pose a question. Asking for a reply takes your "thank you"

from thoughtful note to burdensome corre-
spondence. It's better to keep the messages
separate and send two different emails, one
with a more formal thank you, and one that's
casual and addresses other matters. This
way, your thank you can be received as what
it is: an expression of your gratitude, pure
and simple.

5

OFFER TO HELP

BEING A well-mannered person doesn't mean being meek. You don't have to wait until you're called upon to respond appropriately. Instead, it means keeping an eye out and taking action when your efforts could help someone else. Whether it's at work, at home, or out and about in your town or city, if you spot someone in need, offer your help.

Opportunities to make some else's day a bit easier exist all around us. Volunteer to help someone put their bag into the overhead bin on an airplane; give up your seat on the subway or bus to the elderly, a mother and child, or a pregnant woman; hold the door open for someone else on your way out of a building.

These gestures take mere moments and are a minor inconvenience to you. Yet they have the power to make someone else's day.

The world is a better place when we are reassured that, despite our differences, we are here to help one another. Even when our actions are small, contributing to the good in the world is a powerful thing.

Our prime purpose in this
life is to help others. And if
you can't help them, at least
don't hurt them.

—DALAI LAMA

6

DON'T GOSSIP

GOSSIPING ABOUT other people is tempting entertainment. We don't have to look far to witness other people going on at length about the lives of others. They dish out speculation and judgment about a friend who put on weight after a break-up or a coworker whose marriage is struggling. These items may have some truth to them. But being right about what's going on isn't the point.

Life isn't reality TV and you're not being paid to gossip—and even if you were, talking about other people behind their backs just makes you look petty. Avoid making judgments and sharing your opinion about the way other people speak, act, dress, and live their lives.

Think of the last time you overheard or were informed that someone else was speaking about you behind your back. Did it cause a sinking feeling of disappointment? Did you think to yourself, "But I thought we were friends...?" Once a relationship is undermined in this way, and people begin to second-guess whether they are being treated with respect, a bond is weakened, and it takes significant time and effort before it can be repaired. Don't make the mistake of breaking down your relationships —and your own character—by gossiping.

Rudeness is the weak man's
imitation of strength.

—ERIC HOFFER

7

LISTEN

———————

THERE ARE FEW things that communicate your respect for another person as effectively as listening. Yet, in an era of near-constant distraction, listening well is in danger of becoming a lost art.

Listening seems easy. But true listening requires effort. Keep these things in mind during your next conversation:

Be present in the moment. As you listen to someone else speak, don't distract yourself from what is being said by thinking about your response. Instead, stay in the present moment and really focus on what that person is saying. Trust that the reply will come to you when the time is right; until then, offer your complete attention.

It's okay not to interject. Don't feel compelled to constantly interject with comments while someone else is speaking. Nod your head or smile if you feel it's necessary, but know that your undivided attention speaks volumes.

Maintain eye contact. Even if it's busy in the room or surrounding area, resist the impulse to let your gaze wander. If your phone is on the table, put it in your bag or purse or, at the very least, turn it upside down so the screen isn't visible.

Courage is what it takes to stand up and speak; courage is also what it takes to sit down and listen.

—WINSTON CHURCHILL

Love yourself first and
everything else falls into
line. You really have to love
yourself to get anything
done in this world.

—LUCILLE BALL

8

TREAT YOURSELF WELL

PRACTICING GOOD manners means considering another person's perspective. But it also requires being good to yourself. Think about it: if you are constantly berating or scolding yourself in your own head, how can you practice sensitivity toward those around you?

The next time you find yourself being critical of your appearance, admonishing yourself for a small slip-up you made hours ago, or criticizing yourself for not getting more done, performing better, and acting faster, *stop*. Think of yourself as another person, such as a family member, a dear friend, or a friendly coworker. You wouldn't treat them in such a harsh manner; if you did, they wouldn't want to be around you ever again! So why would you talk to yourself that way? Don't practice bad manners when it comes to how you treat yourself.

9

DON'T ASSUME "HONESTY IS THE BEST POLICY"

THE AGE-OLD MAXIM "honesty is the best policy" is often misunderstood as, "Say whatever is on your mind" or "say what you really think." In truth, there is no reason why the full range of your opinions or feelings should be shared with everyone.

Telling people what you honestly think about who they are, how they look, or what they do may be an honest expression of your opinion, but it won't bring you any closer to anybody—in fact, it will have the opposite effect. People may be admired for their honesty from afar, but who wants to spend time with someone who dishes out razor-sharp criticism in the name of sharing his "honest opinion"?

Having good manners doesn't mean you have to lie or be dishonest. It just means respecting another person's feelings and putting those feelings first. Your honest opinion might save someone from some serious trouble, but if your words will harm, insult, or injure another person, skip it.

Kindness in words creates confidence. Kindness in thinking creates profound- ness. Kindness in giving creates love.

—LAO TZU

10

BE A PERSON
OF YOUR WORD

IF YOU SAY you're going to do something,
do it. This goes for a promise made to a
friend, a task you told a coworker you would
get to before you left for the day, even a piece
of information you told someone you met at a
party that you'd send via email. Even if it's a
small task, treat it with importance. Don't be
someone who lets people down. The world is
full of people who flake out and don't follow
through. But failing to follow up means you
aren't reliable or trustworthy, and people
will think twice before forming a meaningful
personal or working relationship with you.

You want to be remembered as someone
who does what he says. Standing by your
word sets you apart and makes you memora-
ble for all the right reasons.

If you find that keeping your word is consistently difficult for you, keep these things in mind:

Learn to say "no." You may be overpromising, overextending yourself or setting unrealistic expectations for what you can accomplish in a day. Learn to start saying "no" to avoid taking on more than you can handle. Being straightforward and telling someone you can't do something from the outset is preferable to leaving them hanging and giving the impression you'll get something done when you know you can't.

Be realistic about what you say you'll do. Once you've said you'll do something for someone else, create a plan to get it done; if necessary, break the task down into separate steps so you can see exactly what's involved and set aside time accordingly. If it's for a date in the future, use technology to your advantage and set up a reminder on your smart phone or email calendar. If you fail, don't offer excuses. Instead, apologize sincerely.

A man is only as good
as his word.

—PROVERB

11

DON'T EXPECT A "THANK YOU"

WHEN WE OVEREXTEND ourselves for someone else's benefit, it's natural to expect a "thank you" or some other show of appreciation. But sometimes, it doesn't come, and this can be a rude surprise. When another person fails to thank you for your efforts, a gift, or a favor, resist harboring resentment. Avoid spiraling negative thoughts about their character.

Don't dwell on the disappointment that you weren't acknowledged. Realize that, at some point, everyone has done something for someone else and felt that they were underappreciated for it; it's just a part of life.

Instead, feel good about your act of generosity. Take the time to really acknowledge your actions, and give yourself credit for your act of generosity.

What's important is that you continue to reach out to other people and give the best of yourself. Generous behavior is its own reward, and what's more, it is sure to be noticed and appreciated by the people who count.

It's not a slam at you
when people are rude—
it's a slam at the people
they've met before.

—F. SCOTT FITZGERALD

12

TEACH BY EXAMPLE

As YOU WORK on refining your own manners, you may notice that people around you aren't making as much of an effort as you are. Friends may frustrate you with rude behavior like checking their email on their cell phones in the middle of a conversation. Strangers may march through a door you hold open for them without thanking you.

Resist the impulse to glare at a stranger in disapproval or subject a friend to a lecture on etiquette. The most powerful tool of instruction is your own behavior. If your children are behaving rudely, ask yourself if they see you being polite to other adults you encounter on a daily basis, like a waiter, the barista at a cafe, or the cashier at the grocery store. Are you so distracted by tending to your children's needs that you neglect to be polite to other adults by saying "please," "thank you," and "you're welcome?" Kids imitate the behavior they see in the adults closest to them. Practice good manners yourself, and children are sure to follow.

Take the high road. Continue to practice good manners. Your own behavior is sure to influence others and set an example. If you absolutely have to direct someone's attention to their own behavior, express your preferences rather than criticize. Say, "I would really prefer it if you didn't check your email at the dinner table" or, "It would mean so much to me if you were on time the next time we meet." Treating others with consideration is paramount.

Good manners sometimes
means simply putting up with
other people's bad manners.

—H. JACKSON BROWN, JR.

13

DON'T CRITICIZE

At one point or another, each of us has fallen into the trap of thinking that we know what's better for someone else. We may give unsolicited advice or, worse, criticize.

Criticism grates on those around us like an unpleasant noise. It disrupts the delicate intimacy of romantic relationships and causes rifts between friends and family members. And it accomplishes nothing.

Stop yourself from telling someone else how to live her life. Resist the urge to nitpick or be a know-it-all who corrects someone else's behavior. Doing so puts us in a position of superiority. This runs counter to the essence of good manners: being kind and considerate toward others.

No one is perfect. People are permitted their personality quirks and unique preferences without being criticized for them. Even in the case where someone is deliberately rude to you, practice the technique of setting an example rather than becoming negative and critical.

I have no right, by anything I do or say, to demean a human being in his own eyes. What matters is not what I think of him; it is what he thinks of himself. To undermine a man's self-respect is a sin.

—ANTOINE DE SAINT-EXUPERY

14

RESPECT OTHER
PEOPLE'S SPACE

RESPECTING OTHER people's space, liter-
ally and figuratively, is a politeness we often
forget.

At home, respecting other people's space
doesn't just mean giving them privacy when
they ask for it. It also means honoring someone else's silence when they are occupied
with a task, enjoying time alone, or thinking.
If your partner, son, or roommate is in the
middle of a task such as reading or working
online, politely ask if it's a good time for you
to interrupt. If not, ask him if you can revisit
the issue later, and when would be a good
time to do so.

These guidelines are especially important
in the workplace, when people may be in the
middle of a thought or typing an important

email. If someone is in the middle of something when you arrive at their office, either return later or wait by their door or outside their cubicle until they complete their task. Then ask, "Is this a good time?" If not, return later.

Making sure someone is in the right place to receive your message or answer your question ensures that you will enjoy the best communication possible.

When you're out in the world, respecting someone else's space means taking care not to crowd others in close public quarters such as a bus, subway, or crowded restaurant. If you happen to bump into someone, be sure to say, "I'm so sorry," or "Please excuse me." These basic good manners help us get through the day alongside each other.

To be one, to be united is a great thing. But to respect the right to be different is maybe even greater.

—BONO

15

BE APPRECIATIVE

A PPRECIATING THE efforts of others goes beyond writing thank you notes. Practice being appreciative of the efforts of others in your everyday interactions.

When you're out running errands, make a point of making eye contact with a cashier, sales clerk or other employee when you say, "Thank you."

At home, pause for a few moments during the course of a busy day to express your appreciation for the work someone else did to keep the house in order. If you're meeting a friend at a location far from their home, thank them for coming to meet you in your neighborhood. At work, don't wait until the conclusion of a big project to tell someone how much you appreciate his or her contribution to the team. Let them know they're valued.

Expressing appreciation regularly forms the basis of gratitude, a key component to leading a satisfying, joyful, and meaningful life.

The roots of all goodness lie
in the soil of appreciation
for goodness.
—DALAI LAMA

16

AVOID OUTWARD EXPRESSIONS OF FRUSTRATION

HAVING GOOD MANNERS means keeping a cool head no matter what the circumstances. If you're angry, frustrated, or borderline enraged, avoid letting your emotions take over.

Blowing up accomplishes nothing. In fact, it will most likely make it harder for you to solve a problem or get what you want or need.

Furthermore, it's easy to earn a bad reputation, and hard to undo it. No matter how many times you may apologize for your behavior after the fact, the negative impression you made will stick. People are remembered by their actions, and if you lose your cool you'll end up being remembered as "the guy who yelled at his friend at the party" or "the woman who berated the waitress." It's far better to enforce good behavior on yourself in the moment than to make a mistake that will require extensive work to repair your reputation over the long-term.

Remember, it's your choice whether you let your inward emotions spill over into the outward space you share with others. Even when it's difficult, maintain your polite behavior. You'll make things easier on yourself and those around you.

Speak when you are angry
and you will make the best
speech you will ever regret.

—AMBROSE BIERCE

To be idle is a short road to
death and to be diligent is a
way of life; foolish people are
idle, wise people are diligent.

—BUDDHA

17

GET BACK TO PEOPLE PROMPTLY

———

Today we communicate with one another via a variety of means: text messages, chatting online, emails, or a phone call or written letter. With all these ways to be in touch, knowing how soon to reply to someone, whether it's a colleague, friend, family member or acquaintance, can be tricky. When determining how and when to get back to someone, keep a few basic guidelines in mind.

Answer a text with a text, a phone call with a phone call, and so on. Some people are more comfortable with one method over another, and replying to them on their terms shows you're keeping them in mind.

When it comes to getting back to someone within the right timeframe, one great way to determine how long you can politely wait before replying to someone else is to use the speed with which they've replied to you in the past as a gauge. Mimic their timeframe and you will be getting back to them on the terms they are used to.

If you're communicating with someone you've never met, aim to reply within 24 hours. That way they don't have to wonder if their message was lost, and you come across as someone who is prompt and professional.

At work, adhere to the standards imposed by your boss and coworkers. If a message isn't urgent, aim for consistency in how soon you reply. Set a standard that is realistic for you given your workload; whether it's within the hour, by the end of the day, or within 24 hours, aim to stick to it. This way, other people will learn when they can expect to hear back from you. Coworkers, knowing you always reply within a specific timeframe, won't bother with unnecessary follow-up. And you will be relied upon as a person who is consistent in your communication.

Paying attention to how someone else reaches out to you and setting standards for yourself makes polite, effective communication easy and pleasurable.

18

DON'T INTERRUPT

SOMETIMES WE interrupt others without even realizing it. Regardless of your intentions, interrupting someone when he is speaking to you, inserting yourself in a conversation between two people, or talking over a group, is rude and inconsiderate.

Don't interrupt a fight. When misunderstandings arise among family members or friends, it can be tempting to interject with your version of events. As difficult as it may be to listen to two people you love have a tense conversation (and possibly even say mean things to each other), stay out of it. If you interject at the wrong time, you may make things worse by appearing to take sides with one person over the other, and cause a second, ongoing fight. Respect the space that two people have created in their conversation with each other and let them work it out on their own terms, in their own time.

If you're present when someone else is speaking on the phone, don't shout so your voice can be heard in the background or insist on interrupting to get on the line. You'll just create stress for everyone. Instead, let whoever is speaking have her own conversation. If it's a sensitive issue, trust that the two of them will work things out. You don't have to solve everyone else's problems.

During meals or social gatherings, the temptation to correct someone or stand up for ourselves before someone has finished speaking can be too great, and we'll interrupt the conversation to add our own voice. This can lead to meals or gatherings turning into shouting matches.

In each of these situations, use basic good manners to keep yourself in check. Don't make a difficult situation more complicated. Know when to get involved, when it's best to just let things play out, and when to wait until it's your turn to speak.

A man is likely to mind his own business when it is worth minding. When it is not, he takes his mind off his own meaningless affairs by minding other people's business.

—ERIC HOFFER

19

SMILE AND BE FRIENDLY

A SMILE TELLS others who we are without the need to say a word.

In the course of a busy day, we may not have the time to say much beyond "excuse me," "pardon me," or "thank you" to the strangers we encounter. A smile does the job of reassuring others that your apology or appreciation is sincere.

When speaking with people we know at work, at home, or in our neighborhood, smiling before we speak communicates that we are friendly and puts people at ease. A warm, friendly demeanor makes difficult conversations more productive and casual conversations more pleasant.

Begin most of your interactions with other people with a smile and a friendly demeanor.

If you don't receive a smile in return, don't be discouraged. Make an open, pleasant attitude a habit and you will consistently communicate that you have a positive, pleasant personality and are someone worth knowing.

We shall never know all
the good that a simple
smile can do.

—MOTHER TERESA

20

KEEP YOUR PROBLEMS TO YOURSELF

GOING ON AND on about how we feel we were handed the short end of the stick or shortchanged in some way is a bad habit, and bad manners.

When it comes to matters both personal and professional, reciting long lists of what's wrong with your life doesn't bring you closer to anyone. For one thing, it makes for a boring, one-sided conversation. Secondly, people are less inclined to help someone who feels sorry for himself, is self-centered, or comes across as desperate.

Instead of using your time with someone else as an opportunity to dwell on what is wrong with your life, see it as a chance to focus on the positive—for your sake *and* your companions'. Take a break from your worries, anxieties, and complaints.

Talk about what excites and engages you about your life right now. Ask the other person how she's doing and tune in to her responses. Try to enjoy the experience of listening to another person, regardless of what is said. If she starts to talk about her own problems at length, try not to let it bother you. Change the subject when the opportunity arises.

By the end of the conversation, you'll have engaged with your friend in a more meaningful way, and you'll have taken advantage of the chance to set your own problems aside for a while.

Feeling sorry for yourself,
and your present condition,
is not only a waste of energy
but the worst habit you
could possibly have.

—DALE CARNEGIE

Better than a thousand
hollow words, is one word
that brings peace.

—BUDDHA

21

KNOW WHEN TO APOLOGIZE

ALL OF US make mistakes and offend someone else at some point, whether it's at home, among friends, or at work.

Remember that, even if your mistake seems small to you, it's the other person's point of view that matters. Being 10 minutes late might not seem like a big deal to you personally, but when you're meeting an extremely punctual person, it's a problem for her and you need to apologize. Similarly, don't confuse one person's set of standards with another; a 10-minute delay may not be an issue for a friend who is often late himself, but to your other friend, it matters. Be aware of others' personal preferences and strive to adhere to them. If you fail to do so, apologize accordingly.

22

KNOW HOW TO APOLOGIZE MEANINGFULLY

WHEN IT COMES time to make an apology, put the other person first.

Avoid offering a litany of excuses or explanations for your mistakes. If you're writing an email and you find yourself starting your sentences with phrases like, "I had to...," "My boss said...," "My day got so busy...," "I had a last-minute..." realize that you're dwelling too much on yourself for your apology to be effective. Although there may be a long list of things that contributed to your mistake, you alone are responsible for your actions.

Shift your perspective to the other person. What would he want to hear? What will make him feel better? Sometimes a simple "I'm so sorry for changing our plans last-minute" or "Please accept my apologies for canceling again" is all it takes to show someone we care. If we overwhelm them with details about our side of the story, it makes it harder for the other person to tell if we really regret inconveniencing or hurting them.

A stiff apology is a second
insult....The injured
party does not want to
be compensated because
he has been wronged; he
wants to be healed because
he has been hurt.

—G. K. CHESTERTON

23

AVOID PUBLIC PHONE CONVERSATIONS

IT'S A COMMON sight: people talking into their phone as they rush down the street or through a store, speaking to someone else— and subjecting everyone around them to the intimate details of their conversation. Before you pick up your phone to make a call on the go, ask yourself: Do you really want to be *that* person?

Speaking to someone else while you are rushing through your day, navigating busy city streets on foot, or driving, is not only dangerous, it's rude—to both the person with whom you're speaking and those within earshot. You cannot give someone your full attention when half of your mind is occupied with errands. The person on the other end of the line may think it's a personal call taking place in the privacy of your own home and would be disappointed to learn that what they thought was an intimate, one-on-one conversation is background noise for other people. Don't fall into the trap of answering your phone on the go. If you do, or if it's urgent, take the call and inform the person on the other end of the line that you are en route but will make every effort to get to a place where you can speak to them and give them your focused attention. Otherwise, call them back when you're home and can really engage in the conversation.

Without feelings of respect,
what is there to distinguish
men from beasts?
—CONFUCIUS

24

DON'T BOSS

IN STRESSFUL situations where we are trying to accomplish several things in a short period of time, it can be tempting to boss people around to get things done.

In the workplace, we may forget to say "please" or "could you?" and instead just tell someone to do something in a brusque fashion. The same thing may happen at home when we are rushing to get things done.

Remember that bossing people around doesn't guarantee that things will get done faster. In fact, about the only thing it *can* guarantee is that working or teaming up with you will be unpleasant from start to finish. Next time, people may dread working with you or will avoid helping you out.

Once more, treating people rudely can offend them so deeply that you will have to take the time and effort to make it right.

Keep in mind that people aren't robots built to answer commands. Treat those around you with respect, and you'll encourage people to get the job done effectively and efficiently, prevent injured feelings, and ensure you have a group of people who want to work with you the next time around.

The best years of your life
are the ones in which you
decide your problems are
your own. You do not blame
them on your mother, the
ecology, or the president.
You realize that you control
your own destiny.

—ALBERT ELLIS

Too often we underestimate
the power of a touch, a smile,
a kind word, a listening ear,
an honest compliment, or
the smallest act of caring,
all of which have the potential
to turn a life around.

—LEO BUSCAGLIA

25

OFFER A KIND WORD OR GESTURE

OUR LIVES ARE complicated and are often full of unexpected challenges.

Many times, when people are rude, inconsiderate, rushed, or in some way behave without much thought toward others, it's because they are tied up in their own concerns. Some of these concerns may be very serious, such as health problems, worry for a loved one, or a fractured personal relationship.

From people we've only just met to coworkers, friends, and family members, we cannot always be aware of someone's specific circumstances. Even if we know the person well, we can't know the true complexity of what difficulties they're facing. It is best to err on the side of kindness.

We also have demands coming at us from many directions, including work, our personal relationships and our own inner expectations. In short, we have a lot of voices and conflicting priorities telling us what to do and how to do it...on a nearly constant basis.

Offering a kind word, a smile, or if it's someone we know better, a hug if it's appropriate, makes life easier to bear.

PART IV

HELPFUL TIPS
AND GUIDELINES
FOR SOCIAL
SITUATIONS

TABLE MANNERS

Specific rules of conduct at the table vary across cultures around the world.

In the United States, it is generally considered rude to eat with your fingers. But this rule varies around the world, and for different reasons. In Italy, for example, eating prosciutto with your hands is acceptable, as it ensures you can smell the quality of the meat before putting it in your mouth. In Thailand, just a fork and spoon are used, and the fork is only used to put food onto the spoon. Many meat dishes are eaten with the hands. Don't assume that one code of behavior is true across all cultures. Look into it: If you're planning on visiting another country, take the time to briefly research their customs and manners online.

This section provides a brief overview of basic American table manners.

AT THE TABLE: THE BASICS

- Hold your fork with the left hand and the knife with the right.

- Hold the fork with tines down.

- If you're having trouble getting food on your fork, don't use your finger. Instead, use the back of a spoon or the flat side of your knife.

- Never eat directly from the serving bowl. Instead, serve yourself a portion onto your plate and eat from that quantity.

- If a butter dish is on the table, use a butter knife to take a portion of butter from the serving plate and put it onto your own plate, before buttering bread. This prevents the butter dish from getting covered in crumbs and allows you to take the amount of butter you need and pass it along, without making people wait for you.

EATING WITH OTHERS,
AT HOME AND OUT

- If you're dining at someone else's home, do not begin eating until the host or hostess has had the first bite.

- Always serve others before you serve yourself.

- When dining out, always be polite to servers and busboys. A "thank you" is appreciated, as is a tip reflecting the quality of service you received.

- If you need to use the restroom, resist announcing, "I'm gonna go to the bathroom." Simply say, "Please excuse me a moment."

- If you need something slightly out of your reach, you may politely ask someone to pass the item you need ("Please pass the salt."). If the person is speaking or turned away from you and you don't want to interrupt them, it may be preferable to reach for it yourself. Simply say, "Pardon my reach" as you extend your arm for the item.

• If you're eating out, there's an easy way to let your server know whether you are still eating or would prefer that your plate be removed. Think of your plate as a clock. If you're still enjoying your meal and just "resting," place your knife at the top of your plate (blade facing down), with the handle positioned at about four o'clock. Place the fork, tines up and pointed towards the center of the plate, at the bottom, with the handle at around the seven o'clock position. If you are finished eating and ready to have your plate removed, place your utensils together, fork tines up, with the handles between the positions of four and six o'clock. This way, your utensils won't slide off of your plate as it is being removed. A server should not remove your plate if your dining companions are still eating; plates should be cleared when everyone is finished.

RESISTING THE LURE OF YOUR PHONE AT THE DINNER TABLE

When dining with others, never use your cell phone to check your e-mail or text messages or surf online. Although it can be a hard habit to break, doing so is vital to good manners.

Paying more attention to a small machine than the person who sits across from you sends a strong message: "You aren't that important." If that's the message you want to send, why would you bother setting aside the time to be with that person in the first place? Not only does your rude behavior insult those in your company, it shows that you don't take your relationships or the time you spend with others very seriously. This always leaves a bad impression. Far better to wait 30 minutes to check your email or text messages than create a negative impression that can never be undone.

HOW TO BE A GOOD HOST
OR HOSTESS

*Hospitality is making your guests
feel at home, even if you wish
they were.*

—author unknown

———•◦•———

The key to a good party is a good host or
hostess. He or she must be able to make
each guest feel welcome, put guests at ease
amongst each other, and provide an environment that is amenable to conversation
and fun.

If you're hosting the party, keep these tips
in mind:

• The moment someone arrives, thank him
  for coming and let him know how great it
  is to see him.

• If appropriate and genuine, pay your
  guest a compliment. If your party is a

formal affair, or a dress-up party, this will be especially appreciated, as your guests most likely put time and effort into their appearance.

- Offer to take their coats, and offer them refreshments or snacks right away. If you are too occupied to get them a drink, point them in the direction of the kitchen or bar and say, "Please, help yourself to a drink and I'll be over to join you shortly."

- When conversing with your guests, add details that make reference to the last time you spoke or communicated by saying something such as, "I can't wait to hear about the new puppy!" or "I haven't seen you in so long, I'm so excited to hear about things at the new apartment!" Little details like this show that you are involved and interested in your friends' lives and will make it easy to pick up the conversation when you return to them later.

HOW TO BE A GOOD GUEST

*At a dinner party one should eat
wisely but not too well, and talk well
but not too wisely.*

—W. Somerset Maugham

———•••———

Being a good guest begins with the way you respond to an invitation. Even if you receive a casual email or a text message that doesn't ask for an RSVP, always reply. Being the recipient of an invitation means that someone thought of you fondly and took the time to reach out to request that you join their event. Don't sour their good feelings about you by failing to acknowledge their kindness. Even if you're not yet sure if you can attend, be sure to acknowledge the invitation so the other person doesn't have to follow up. Responding only takes a few moments, and with all the ways we have to be in touch, there really isn't any excuse for not replying. Being invited to attend an event is an honor not to be taken lightly. Take care to reply to any invitation; otherwise you may not receive one again.

When it comes to attending a party or event, ask yourself: How do you want to be remembered by the host and other guests? It may be easy to just keep to yourself and the people you know, but do you want to be remembered as someone who showed up, snacked on free food and enjoyed free beverages, only hung out with the people you came with, and left?

Consider how much more enriching the experience would be, both for you and everyone around you, if you helped out and gave back in a social setting. Starting new conversations and being open and friendly is genuinely appreciated. Keep in mind, too, that it takes a tremendous amount of work to host a social gathering in one's home. As a thank you to the host, offer to help clean up or make the effort to be sure any plates or cups you used are disposed of properly. Chipping in to make the work easier offers a meaningful "thank you."

ARRIVING AND GREETINGS

As a guest, your arrival and departure give you your primary opportunities to connect directly with your host and show your appreciation.

It is always advisable to bring something with you for the host, whether it's drinks or food for everyone to enjoy, or flowers or a small gift (for a housewarming or other special occasion). Smile and immediately express your gratitude at being invited, or say, "It's so good to see you!" From there, your host should invite you in and welcome you to help yourself to food and drinks. He or she may be occupied for most of the evening but will likely come over to speak with you and make introductions as the party goes on. If the host is a close friend, feel free to offer to help out or lend a hand if it seems it would give him more time to enjoy himself.

LEAVING AND GOOD-BYES

At the end of a long evening, it can be tempting to leave a party without saying good-bye to the host. This is extremely rude and will generally be remembered if the gathering was small ("Did so-and-so leave without saying good-bye?" your host will ask himself the next day). A parting word takes only a few minutes, and there is no excuse for skipping it.

If the host or hostess is in the middle of speaking to a large group of people, stand outside the group for a few moments and wait for the right moment to interrupt. Gently tap your host on the shoulder and quickly say, "I/we had such a lovely time, thank you so much." Leave it up to your host to take a few minutes apart from the other guests for a longer good-bye. Even if it's brief, your kind words of appreciation will be remembered.

If you'd like to say good-bye to other people you met at the party, try:

- "I'm glad we met!"
- "I enjoyed meeting you!"
- "I hope to see you again."

You can add details about something that person said earlier, such as:

- "Have a great time at the movie tomorrow night!"
- "Enjoy your vacation next week!"
- Good luck with the new job!"

If someone says they enjoyed meeting you, don't just say, "Thanks!" Reply with:

- "Same here!"
- "Likewise."
- "As did I."
- "It was great to meet you, too! I'm so glad we had the opportunity to talk about [topic]."

TIPS FOR MORE ENJOYABLE CONVERSATION

Good manners is the art of making those people easy with whom we converse. Whoever makes the fewest people uneasy is the best bred in the room.

—Jonathan Swift

————•·•————

Some people are at their best around others and seem to be equally at ease among strangers as among friends. They move easily from group to group, chatting about a variety of topics.

Others struggle to interject themselves and hang out at the edge of a party or social gathering. In cases of "conversational paralysis," sometimes an easy way out is to stop focusing on yourself. For example, work to stop dwelling on concerns like, "What do they think of me? How do I look?" Think instead how you can put someone *else* at ease or start a fun conversation. Sometimes the way out of your own shyness is to stop spending so much time thinking about yourself, and shift your attention to those around you. Most likely, other guests are feeling shy, too, and your openness will be a relief to them.

FOR THE HOST
(INTRODUCING GUESTS
TO EACH OTHER)

If you're introducing one guest to another, provide the start to a longer conversation by saying:

"[Name] loves to [sail, cook, collect vinyl records, read] just like you."

FOR THE GUEST
(INTRODUCING YOURSELF)

If no one introduces you and you've just arrived, try a friendly:

"We haven't met, have we? My name is [Name]."

If you encounter someone you've met before, but whose name you can't recall, don't play a game where you present him or her to another person to try to get them to announce their name to someone else.

Instead simply say, "I apologize, but your name has slipped my mind. Could you please remind me?" or "I'm so sorry, but I seem to have forgotten your name. Would you please refresh my memory?"

KEEPING THE CONVERSATION BALL ROLLING

If you're being introduced and you know the person's name, instead of saying, "I've heard so much about you!" try "My [friend/coworker/person making introductions] says that you [make the best quiches, sailed across the Atlantic, recently got back from New Zealand], etc."

When another person enters the conversation, try:

"[Name] and I were just talking about [topic]. What do you think?" or "Have you ever been?," etc.

If you say you're going to do something for someone, or you mention getting together on another occasion, exchange information and follow up. There's simply no excuse for not keeping your word. If you fail, you risk spoiling a new relationship that could be pleasant or mutually beneficial. You never know when you may run into that person again, and it's best not to leave the impression that you are unreliable or flaky.

CONCLUSION

To a large extent, our lives are made up of interactions with the people around us.

Sometimes we forget this. We think that life is about being perfect or enjoying a stress-free existence. But sooner or later reality reminds us that, no matter how well prepared we may be, things don't always go as we planned, and no one is perfect.

What is remarkable is how much we can enjoy our lives with each other in spite of its stresses, challenges, and upheavals. Ultimately, what is often most rewarding is the way we spend time together. From a brief exchange with a neighbor in the morning, a conversation with a coworker over lunch, or a walk with a loved one, our lives are made up of moments with one another.

Manners help us make the most of those moments. They remind us to keep a cool head when a minor annoyance arises, refrain from criticizing someone, or hold back from going on at length about our frustrating day. With these interruptions set aside, we can enjoy a more meaningful encounter with others.

Behaving politely also helps us put our best foot forward. The way we interact with others forms a portrait in their minds of who we are. If we are considerate and enthusiastic, we will be remembered that way. If we are rude or short-tempered, we will be thought of in a negative light. Manners help us be our best selves.

Manners are more than just a set of tools we can use to get ahead. They enrich our experience of living and the time we spend with each other.

ABOUT
NORAH LAWLOR

Norah Lawlor is the Founder and Principal of Lawlor Media Group Inc., a New York-based boutique strategy PR firm focused on a luxury lifestyle clientele ranging from not-for-profit to real estate, hospitality, travel, and entertainment. She lives in New York City and has both written and contributed to a range of publications on the social and society scene in New York, the Hamptons, and internationally.